Monica Russel is an experienced knitter with many original designs to her credit. She regularly has her designs published in Simply Knitting and Knit Now, and has written a number of books full of her creative knitting patterns. See the inside back page for further details.

Monica also runs knitting workshops and can often be seen at craft fairs and exhibitions around the United Kingdom.

For more information please visit her website at:

www.theknitknacks.co.uk

Book design and photography by Simon Bartrum, photographer. Visit his website at:

www.photosimon.net

ISBN 978-1-78456-511-4

Introduction

Cosies are fun and practical. They can be used to keep tea-pots, cafétières and eggs warm and make a great display in the kitchen. All the tea-cosies, except for the Baby Ribbed, fit a 4 cup teapot.

Each cosy comes with a full set of instructions and can be made in a weekend. Charts are included where necessary and the more complex stitches are explained in the knitter's notes.

The designs are inspired by nature with colours that can be adapted to your individual choice.

For all these patterns Rooster's Almerino Aran is used, partly because of the colours and the way they blend together, and also because they are made from natural fibres. The yarn is a standard gauge so could be substituted by one of your choice.

All the yarns for these projects and kits can be ordered from the website.

www.theknitknacks.co.uk

Contents

Abbreviations

K	:	Knit
P	:	Purl
K2(3)tog	:	Knit two (three) together
RS	:	Right Side
WS	:	Wrong Side
st(s)	:	Stitch (stitches)
sl 1	:	Slip 1
tbl	:	Through back of loop
psso	:	Pass slipped stitch over
rep	:	Repeat
dpns	:	Double-pointed needles
MB	:	Make bobble

Notes for Knitters

'I' Cord

- With right side facing and chosen colour, K5, (or specified no of sts).

- Without turning slide sts to the opposite end of the needle and bring the yarn to the opposite end of your work pulling it quite tightly across the wrong side of the knitting.

- Knit these stitches again and repeat this process 5 times more (or specified number in pattern). Cast off stitches.

Stranding Yarn (For Intarsia or pattern repeats where two or more colours are used).

- Twist yarn every two – three sts to avoid large loops at the back of work.

- Always twist the yarn on the first and last stitch of the motif and the main colour so there is no gap between the colour changes.

Making A Bobble

- Make Bobble: (k1, yo, k1, yo, k1) into next stitch, turn and p5, turn and k1, Sl 1, k2tog, psso, k1, turn and p3 tog (bobble completed).

- Turn, (RS facing) Knit into the bobble stitch again with the bobble colour.

Casting on

- Next row, when using a traditional casting on, knit into the back of each stitch (this will form a neat edge).

Vintage Ruched

An old favourite that could be seen in many households in the 1950'S.
The ruching adds texture to the cosy and the density will keep your
brew warm for a long time.

Materials

You will need:

- A pair of 4.5mm (UK 7/US 7) knitting needles
- A pair of 5mm (UK 6/US 8) knitting needles
- Two 4.5mm double pointed needles

- 2 x 50g ball of Aran Weight Yarn 65% Wool, 35% Alpaca, 94m (103yds)
- Suggested colours:
    - Cornish (A)
    - Rooster (B)

Tension

'arn knits as Aran to this tension: 19sts and 23rows to measure 10 x 0cm (4 x 4in) over st st using 5mm needles.

'lease check tension before starting this project.

Knitting The Cosy (2 Identical pieces)

Using size 4.5mm needles and yarn A cast on 62sts.
Change to 5mm needles

1. Row 1: Slip 1A, * K5B, K5A, rep from * to last st, K1B
2. Row 2: S1B, * Put yarn A to the front (RS), and yarn B to the back, K5A, Put yarn A to the back and yarn B to the front, K5B, repeat from * to last stitch, K1 A
3. Repeat these 2 rows until piece measures 16.5cm (6.25in).
4. Cut off yarn A

Decreasing For The Crown

5. Row 1: * K1, K3tog, rep from * to last 2 sts, K2 (32sts)
6. Row 2: K2tog, *K1, P1, rep from * to last 2sts, K2tog
7. Row 3: *K1, sl 1, K1 psso, rep from * to end (20sts)
8. Row 4: Knit
9. Row 5: *K2tog, rep from * to end (10sts)
10. Row 6: P1, *P3tog, rep from * to end.
11. Make an 8 row I cord

To Make Up

12. With right sides facing join the bottom edges for approx 1.5cm (0.75in).
13. Sew your side seams leaving sufficient space for the spout at one side and the handle on the other side.
14. Sew in loose ends by weaving them into the back of your work.
15. Join the I cords at the bottom.

Dog Tea Cosy

This pattern practices the skills of intarsia and gives you the opportunity for textured knitting. The tea cosy will fit a standard 4 cup teapot. Change the suggested colours to suit your taste. The body of the cosy is knitted in one background colour.

Materials

- A pair of 4.5mm (UK 7/US 7) knitting needles
- A pair of 5mm (UK 6/US 8) knitting needles
- Two 4.5mm double pointed needles

- 1 x 50g ball of Aran Weight Yarn 65% Wool, 35% Alpaca, 94m (103yds) for background
- Part balls of contrasting colours

- Suggested colours:
    - Rooster (A) (background)
    - Caviar (B) (motif)
    - Cornish (2 metres) (C) (tail)

Tension

Yarn knits as Aran to this tension: 19sts and 23rows to measure 10 x 10cm (4 x 4in) over st st using 5mm needles.

Knitting The Cosy (2 Identical pieces)

1. Using size 4.5mm needles and yarn A cast on 41sts.
2. Row 1: *K2, P2, rep from * to last st, K1
3. Row 2: P1 *K2, P2, rep from * to end
4. Repeat these 2 rows once more.
5. Change to 5mm needles
6. Rows 5-12: Stocking stitch
7. Rows 13-28: Work from chart
8. Rows 29-32: Stocking stitch
9. Rows 33-34: Knit
10. Row 35: *K1, P1, rep from * to last stitch, K1
11. Row 36: P1, * K1, P1, rep from * to end
12. Rows 37-38: Knit
13. Work at this point should measure 16.5cm (6.5in)

Decreasing For The Crown

14. Row 1: *P3tog, K1, rep from * to last st, K1 (21sts)
15. Row 2: *K1, P1, rep from * to last st, K1
16. Row 3: K1, *sl 1, K1 psso, rep from * to end (11sts)
17. Row 4: Purl to last 2 sts, P2tog (10sts)
18. Row 5: *K2tog, rep from * to end
19. Cut off yarn A
20. Slip rem 5 sts onto a double pointed needle and work a 20 row I cord, using colour B.
21. Cast off sts.

To Make Up

22. With right sides facing join ribs at the bottom of the cosy.
23. Sew your side seams leaving sufficient space for the spout at one side and the handle on the other side.
24. Sew in loose ends by weaving them into the back of your work.
25. Fold I cord in half to form a loop and sew into place.

Dog motif :

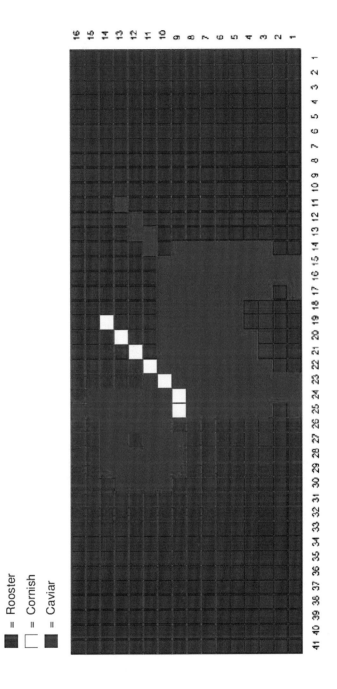

= Rooster
= Cornish
= Caviar

Fleur

This is one of the more classical tea cosies and would look great on display in the kitchen, ready for use when you have tea with family or friends.
This cosy will give you the opportunity to practice working from charts.

Materials

- A pair of 4.5mm (UK 7/US 7) knitting needles
- A pair of 5mm (UK 6/US 8) knitting needles
- Pom-pom maker or cardboard to make pom-pom

- 1 x 50g ball of Aran Weight Yarn 65% Wool, 35% Alpaca, 94m (103yds)
- Part balls of two contrasting colours
- Suggested colours:
    - Cornish (A)
    - Gooseberry (B)
    - Sorbet (C)

Tension

Yarn knits as Aran to this tension: 19sts and 23rows to measure 10 x 10cm (4 x 4in) over st st using 5mm needles.
Please check tension before starting this project.

Knitting The Cosy (2 Identical pieces)

1. Using size 4.5mm needles and yarn A cast on 41sts.
2. Row 1: P1 *K1, P1, rep from * to end
3. Repeat these 2 rows once more.
4. Change to 5mm needles
5. Rows 5-6: Stocking stitch, colour B
6. Rows: 7- 30: Work from chart
7. Rows: 31-40: Stocking stitch, colour A.
8. Work at this point should measure 16cm (6.25in)

Decreasing For The Crown

9. Row 1: *P3tog, K1, rep from * to last st, K1 (21sts)
10. Row 2: *K1, P1, rep from * to last st, K1
11. Row 3: K1, *sl 1, K1 psso, rep from * to end (11sts)
12. Row 4: Purl to last 2 sts, P2tog (10sts)
13. Row 5: *K2tog, rep from * to end (5sts)

Pom-pom

14. Make a pom-pom using colours B and C (one strand of each).
15. Run a needle through remaining 10 sts (5 from each side) at top of the cosy and fasten off.

To Make Up

16. With right sides facing join the ribs at the bottom of the cosy.
17. Sew your side seams leaving sufficient space for the spout at one side and the handle on the other side.
18. Sew in loose ends by weaving them into the back of your work.
19. Sew your pom-pom on top of the cosy.

Fleur motif:

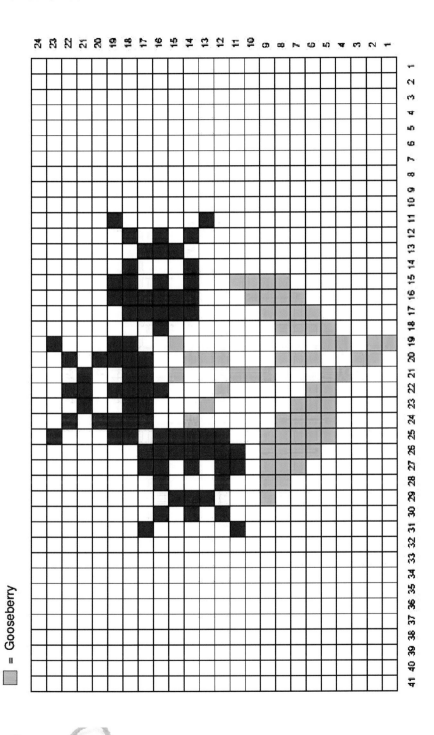

Sheep

This great tea cosy won't pull the wool over their eyes. Not only will it keep your teapot warm but it will also liven up your table. The chart is easy to follow and gives you all the help you need to knit the sheep.

Materials

- Two 4.5mm double pointed needles
- A pair of 4.5mm (UK 7/US 7) knitting needles
- A pair of 5mm (UK 6/US 8) knitting needles
- Pom-pom maker or cardboard to make pom-pom

- 2 x 50g balls of Aran Weight Yarn 65% Wool, 35% Alpaca, 94m (103yds)
- Suggested colours:
    - 1 ball Gooseberry (A)
    - 1 ball Cornish (B)
    - Small amount Caviar

Tension

1. Yarn knits as Aran to this tension: 19sts and 23rows to measure 10 x 10cm (4 x 4in) over st st using 5mm needles.
2. Please check tension before starting this project.

Knitting The Cosy (2 Identical pieces)

3. Using size 4.5mm needles and yarn A cast on 39sts.
4. Row 1: *K2, P2, rep from * to last st P1.
5. Row 2: K1 *P2, K2, rep from * to end
6. Repeat these 2 rows once more.
7. Change to 5mm needles
8. Rows 5-12: Stocking stitch
9. Start working from the grid. Cut off yarns B and C when the motif is complete.
10. Rows 29-40: stocking stitch, colour A.

Decreasing For The Crown

11. Row 1: K1 (p3 tog, k1) 9 times, K2 (21sts)
12. Row 2: K1, *k1, p1, rep from * to end
13. Row 3: K1, *sl 1, K1 psso, rep from * to end (11sts)
14. Row 4: Purl to last 2 sts, P2tog (10sts)
15. Row 5: K3tog X 2, K2tog x 2 (4sts)
16. Cut off yarn A

Pom-pom

17. Make a pom-pom using Caviar
18. Run a needle through 8 sts left at top of the cosy and fasten off. Join your pom-pom to the top of the cosy.

To Make Up

19. With right sides facing join the ribs at the bottom of the cosy.
20. Sew your side seams leaving sufficient space for the spout at one side and the handle on the other side.
21. Sew in loose ends by weaving them into the back of your work.

Sheep motif:

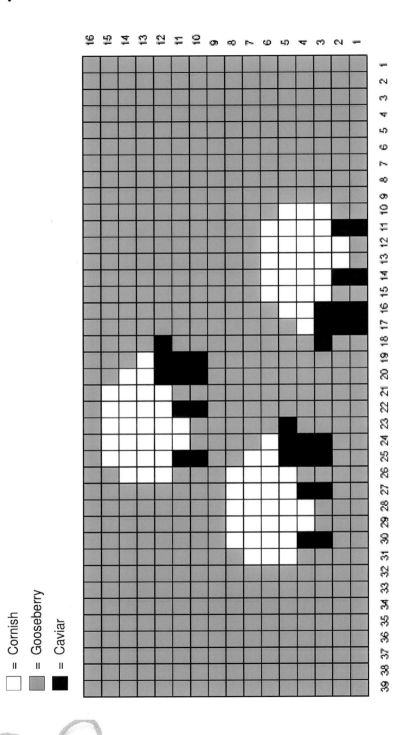

☐ = Cornish

▨ = Gooseberry

■ = Caviar

At the Seaside

This tea cosy reminds me of an old-fashioned seaside scene with beach huts. I have chosen pastel colours but strong colours would work equally well.

Materials

- A pair of 4.5mm (UK 7/US 7) knitting needles
- A pair of 5mm (UK 6/US 8) knitting needles
- Two double pointed 4.5 (UK 7/US 7) needles

- 1 x 50g ball of Aran Weight Yarn 65% Wool, 35% Alpaca, 94m (103yds) (background)
- Part balls of three contrasting colours

- Suggested colours:
    - (A) Sugared Almond
    - (B) Cornish
    - (C) Strawberries and cream
    - (D) Grape

Tension

1. Yarn knits as Aran to this tension: 19sts and 23rows to measure 1C x 10cm (4 x 4in) over st st using 5mm needles.
2. Please check tension before starting this project.

Knitting The Cosy (2 Identical pieces)

3. Using size 4.5mm needles and yarn A cast on 41sts.
4. Row 1: *K1, P1, rep from * to last st, K1
5. Row 2: P1 *K1, P1, rep from * to end
6. Rows 3-4: Knit
7. Rows 5-6: As rows 1 and 2
8. Change to 5mm needles
9. Rows 5-8: Stocking stitch
10. Rows 9-28: Work from chart
11. Rows 29-34: Stocking stitch
12. Row 35: *K1, P1, rep from * to last st, K1
13. Row 36: P1 *K1, P1, rep from * to end
14. Repeat rows 35 -36 twice more
15. Work at this point should measure 16cm (6.25in) at this point.

Decreasing For The Crown

16. Row 1: *K3tog, P1, rep from * to last st, K1 (21sts)
17. Row 2: *P1, K1, rep from * to last st, P1
18. Row 3: K1, *sl 1, K1 psso, rep from * to end (11sts)
19. Row 4: P2tog, P3, P2tog, P2, P2tog
20. Row 5: *K2tog, rep from * to end (4sts)
21. Cut off yarn A
22. Using yarn B, slide your 4 sts onto a double pointed needles.
23. Make a 12 row I cord

To Make Up

24. With right sides facing join the ribs at the bottom of the cosy.
25. Sew your side seams leaving sufficient space for the spout at one side and the handle on the other side.
26. Join the I cord by tying it together.
27. Sew in loose ends by weaving them into the back of your work.

Seaside motif:

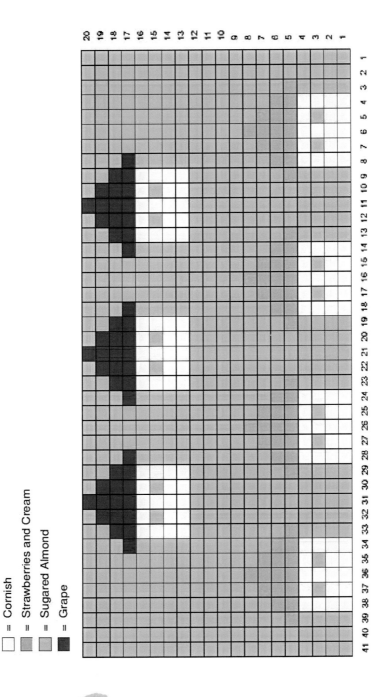

= Cornish
= Strawberries and Cream
= Sugared Almond
= Grape

Funky Bobble

This is a fun and funky tea cosy using garter and stocking stitch with staggered bobbles. Use two colours that really contrast although it will look good in any colour combination you fancy. It also works well in one colour.

Materials

- A pair of 4.5mm (UK 7/US 7) knitting needles
- A pair of 5mm (UK 6/US 8) knitting needles
- 2 x 50g ball of Aran Weight Yarn 65% Wool, 35% Alpaca, 94m (103yds)
- Suggested colours
  - Custard (A)
  - Sorbet (B)

Tension

1. Yarn knits as Aran to this tension: 19sts and 23rows to measure 10 x 10cm (4 x 4in) over st st using 5mm needles.
2. Please check tension before starting this project.

Knitting The Cosy (2 Identical pieces)

3. Using size 4.5mm needles and yarn A cast on 38sts.
4. Rows 1-4: *K1, P1, rep from * to end
5. Change to 5mm needles
6. Rows 5-6: Stocking stitch
7. Rows 7-8: Knit
8. Rows 9-12: Stocking stitch
9. Row 13: K4A * MB colour B, K1A, MB colour B, K6, rep from * to last 7sts, MB, K1A, MB, K4A
10. Rows 14: Purl
11. Row 15: K5A, *MB using colour B, K8, rep from * to last 6sts, MB using colour B, K5
12. Rows 16-18: Stocking stitch starting with a purl row.
13. Rows 19-20: Knit
14. Rows 21-24: Stocking stitch
15. Row 25: K4A * MB colour B, K1A, MB colour B, K6, rep from * to last 7sts, MB, K1A, MB K4A
16. Rows 26: Purl
17. Row 27: K5A, *MB using colour B, K8, rep from * to last 6sts, MB using colour B, K5
18. 28 – 30: Stocking stitch starting with a purl
19. Rows 31-32: Knit
20. Rows 33–36: Stocking stitch
21. Row 37: K4A * MB colour B, K1B, MB colour B, K6, rep from * to last 7sts, MB, K1A, MB, K4A
22. Row 38: Purl
23. Row 39: K5A, *MB using colour B, K8, rep from * to last 6sts, MB using colour B, K5
24. Row 40: Purl

Decreasing For The Crown

25. Row 1: * K3, K2tog, rep from* to last 3sts, K3 (31sts)
26. Row 2: Purl to last 2sts, P2tog (30sts)
27. Row 3: * K2, K2tog, rep to last 2sts, K2 (23sts)
28. Row 4: Knit
29. Row 5: *K3tog, rep to last 2sts, K2tog (8sts)
30. Place rem sts on a holder
31. Make two small pom-poms in yarn B

To Make Up

32. Run a needle through remaining 16sts (8 from each side) at top of the cosy and fasten off.
33. With right sides facing join the ribs at the bottom of the cosy.
34. Sew your side seams leaving sufficient space for the spout at one side and the handle on the other side.
35. Sew your two pom-poms onto the top of the cosy.
36. Sew in loose ends by weaving them into the back of your work.

Baby Ribbed

This ribbed tea cosy is a very quick knit. Either treat yourself to new yarns or purchase my kit.

Materials

- A pair of 4.5mm (UK 7/US 7) knitting needles
- A pair of 5mm (UK 6/US 8) knitting needles
- Two 4.5mm double pointed needles
- Pom-pom maker or cardboard for making pom-pom (optional)
- 3 x 25g of Aran Weight Yarn 65% Wool, 35% Alpaca
- Suggested colours
    - Grape (A)
    - Gooseberry (B)
    - Sorbet (C)

Tension

1. Yarn knits as Aran to this tension: 19sts and 23rows to measure 10 x 10cm (4 x 4in) over st st using 5mm needles.
2. Please check tension before starting this project.

Knitting The Cosy (2 Identical pieces)

3. Using size 4.5mm needles and yarn A cast on 30sts.
4. Row 1: *K3A, P3A, rep from * to end.
5. Rep row 1 three more times then change to 5mm needles.
6. Cont working in 4 row stripes of each colour until piece measures 12.5cm (5in).

Shaping the Top

7. Row 1: *K3tog, K1, rep from *to last 2sts, K2 (16sts)
8. Row 2: *K1, P1, rep from * to end
9. Row 3:*Sl 1, K1, psso, rep from * to end (8sts)
10. Slip 4 sts onto a double pointed needle and using yarn B make a seven row I cord, fasten.
11. Slip rem 4 sts onto a double pointed needle and make a 2nd I cord as the first one, using yarn C.

Pom-pom Variation

12. Run a needle through 8 sts left at top of the cosy and fasten off. Join your pom-pom to the top of the cosy.

To Make Up

13. With right sides facing join the ribs at the bottom of the cosy.
14. Join the I cords at the crown of the cosy, sew your side seams leaving sufficient space for the spout at one side and the handle on the other side.
15. Sew in loose ends by weaving them into the back of your work.

Tea with roses

This cable cosy will keep your brew lovely and warm. By using the yarn double it will be chunky and the cables will stand out beautifully. Go for a neutral colour with bright roses, or mix and match your favourite shades.

Materials

- A pair of 4.5mm needles
- A pair of 5mm needles
- 1 cable needle

- Rooster's Almerino Aran (50% baby alpaca, 50% merino, 50g, 94m (103yds)
- Suggested Colours

  - 2 balls Silver (colour A)
  - Part ball Sorbet (colour B)
  - Part ball Damson (colour C)

Tension

1. Yarn knits as Aran to this tension: 20sts and 25rows to measure 10 x 10cm (4 x 4in) over st st using 4.5 mm needles.
2. Please check tension before starting this project.

Knitting The Cosy

Roses (Make 4)

3. Cast on 84sts using 5mm needles and yarn B or C
4. Row 1: Ktbl into every stitch to form a neat edge.
5. Row 2: (P2tog) to end (42sts)
6. Row 3: Knit
7. Row 4: *p2tog, p4, rep from * to end of row (35sts)
8. Row 5: Knit
9. Row 6: (P2tog) to last st, P1. (18sts)
10. Row 7: Knit
11. Row 8: *P2tog , rep to end of row (9sts)
12. Cut yarn and thread through rem sts, drawing into a spiral flower

Tea Cosy (Make 2)

Note that the body of the tea cosy is knitted with the yarn held double throughout.
13. Cast on 44sts using 4.5mm needles and colour A held double.
14. Next row Ktbl to end
15. Change to 5 mm needles

Cable Pattern

16. Row 1: P2 * K4, P2, rep from * to end
17. Rows 2 and 4: K2, * P4, K2, rep from * to end
18. Row 3: P2, *C4B, P2, rep from * to end
19. Repeat the above 4 rows until work measures 6.5ins (16cms), ending on a row 2 or 4.

Decreasing For The Crown

20. Row 1: P2* K2tog, K2, P2tog, K2, K2tog,P2 rep from * to last 6sts, K2tog, K2, P2tog (33sts)
21. Row 2: K1 * P3, K2, P3, K1, rep from * to last 5sts, P3, K2
22. Row 3: *K2tog, rep from * to last st,K1 (17sts)
23. Row 4: Purl
24. Row 5: *K2tog, rep from * to last st, K1 (9sts)
25. Row 6: Purl
26. Cut yarn leaving a long tail for sewing up.
27. Using a tapestry needle thread yarn tail through remaining sts on your needle.

To Make Up

28. Using a mattress stitch secure the top of the cosy. Using a mattress stitch with RS facing sew up each side leaving a space for the spout and the handle.
29. With right sides facing join the ribs at the bottom of the cosy.
30. Sew on your 4 roses alternating colours.
31. Weave all ends into the back of the cosy.

Cafétière and Mug cuffs

These are fun and functional projects that are simple to make and will help you to keep your coffee lovely and warm whether in the cafétière or in a favourite mug. Spots are fun and you can use different colours for each member of the family.

Materials

- A pair of 5mm needles
- Rooster's Aran (50% baby alpaca/50% Merino Wool 50g, 94m (103yds)
- Suggested colours
  - One ball of each:
  - Yarn A Strawberries and Cream
  - Yarn B Cornish

Tension

1. Yarn knits as Aran to this tension: 22sts and 22rows to measure 10 x 10cm (4 x 4in) over st st using 5 mm needles.
2. Please check tension before starting this project.

Cafétière Cover (18cm (7in) cafétière)

3. Using 5mm needles and yarn A cast on 40sts.
4. Next row ktbl
5. Row 1: *K1,P1 rep from * to end
6. Row 2: * P1, K1, rep from * to end
7. Repeat rows 1 and 2 once more
8. Row 5: Knit
9. Row 6: Purl
10. Row 7: K3A, * K2B, K6A, rep from * to last 5sts, K2B, K3A
11. Row 8: P2A, * P4A, P4B, rep from * to last 2sts, P2A
12. Row 9: K2A, * K4B, K4A, rep from * to last 6sts, K4B, K2A
13. Row 10: P3A, *P2B, P6A, rep from * to last 5sts, P2B, P3A
14. Row 11: Knit in A
15. Row 12: Purl in A
16. Row 13: K7A, * K2B, K6A, rep from * to last 9sts, K2B, K7A
17. Row 14: P6A, * P4B, P4A, rep from * to last 10sts, P4B, P6A
18. Row 15: K6A, * K4B, K4A, rep from * to last 6sts, K6A
19. Row 16: P7A, *P2B, P6A, rep from *to last 9sts, P2B, P7A
20. Continue working the 12 row pattern (rows 5 -16) until work measures approx 31cm (12in) from cast on edge and where you have completed 2 rows of st st either in the middle of the dots or the end of the sequence.
21. Cut off yarn B
22. Work rows 1-2 twice
23. Cast off sts

Ties (Make 6)

24. Using 5mm needles and yarn B cast on 14sts
25. Rows 1-3: Knit Cast off sts
26. Sew cast-on edge to cast-off edge to form a cord.

To Make Up

27. Sew one tie on each side of top of cafétière cover.
28. Sew one strap on each side of middle of the cafétière
29. Sew one tie at each side of bottom of the cafétière.
30. Wrap the main body of knitting around your cafétière and knot up cords to secure it.
31. Sew in loose ends.
32. Note: You will have sufficient yarn leftover to make one mug cuff with B as the main colour.

Mug Cuff 1 (For a 10cm (4in) high mug)

1. Using 5mm needles and yarn B cast on 22sts
2. Next row ktbl
3. Row 1: *K1,P1 rep from * to end
4. Row 2: * P1, K1, rep from * to end
5. Row 3: Knit
6. Row 4: K1, purl to last st, K1
7. Row 5: K2B, * K2A, K6B, rep from * to last 4sts, K2A, K2B
8. Row 6: K1B, * P4A P4B, rep from * until last 5sts, P4A, K1B
9. Row 7: K1B, *K4A, K4B, rep from * to last 5sts, K4A, K1B,
10. Row 8: K1B, P1B * P2A, P6B, rep from * to last 4sts, P2A, P1B, K1B
11. Row 9: Knit
12. Row 10: K1B, purl to last st, K1B
13. Row 11: K6B, * K2A, K6B, rep from * to last 8sts, K2A, K6B
14. Row 12: K1B P4B * P4A, P4B, rep from * to last 9sts, P4A, P4B,K1B
15. Row 13: K5B, * K4A, K4B, rep from * to last 5sts, K5B
16. Row 14: K1B, P5B, P2A, P6B, P2A, P5B, K1B
17. Continue working the 12 row pattern (rows 3 -14) until work measures approx 22cm (8.75in) from cast on edge and where you have completed 2 rows of st st either in the middle of the dots or the end of the sequence.
18. Cut off yarn B
19. Work rows 1-2 once
20. Cast off sts

Mug Cuff 2

21. As mug cuff 1 reversing your colours.

Ties

22. Make 4 in Yarn A as for Cafétière

To Make Up

23. Sew one tie at each side of the cast on edge and one tie at each end of cast off edge. Sew in ends

What could be more useful than a cosy to keep that breakfast egg warm while you butter your toast!

Egg cup cosies

Materials (for all cosies)

- A pair of 5mm (UK 6/US 8) knitting needles
- A pom-pom maker or a piece of card to make the pom-poms
- Two 4.5 double pointed needles to make the I cords.

Bobble Egg Cosy

Simply choose two colours: for the main colour you will need approximately 13m and for the second colour approximately 7m.

Cut lengths of 2 metres of contrasting yarn for each bobble row.

1. Using 5mm needles and yarn A cast on 28sts.
2. Foundation row (only if using the traditional cast on method), ktbl
3. Rows 1 and 2: * K2, P2, rep from * to end
4. Rows 5–8: Stocking stitch
5. Row 9: K3A, * MB using colour B, K6A, rep from * to last 4 sts MB, K3A
6. Rows 10–12: Stocking stitch starting with a purl row
7. Row 13: K6A, MB, K6A, MB, K7A, MB, K6A
8. Rows 14–16: Stocking stitch starting with a purl row
9. Row 17: * K2tog, rep from * to end
10. Row 18: Purl
11. Row 19: * K2tog, rep from * to end
12. Cut off yarn leaving enough yarn to thread your needle through the remaining sts and gather them together and then to sew up the side seam of the egg cosy.
13. Make a pom-pom to go on the top of the cosy.

Striped Egg Cosy

This striped egg cosy a very quick project and can be made with any yarn leftovers.

1. Using 5mm needles and yarn A cast on 28sts.
2. Foundation row (only if using the traditional cast on method), ktbl
3. Rows 1-4: Knit yarn A
4. Rows 5-8: Stocking stitch yarn B
5. Rows 9-12: Stocking stitch yarn C
6. Rows 13-16: Stocking stitch yarn A
7. Row 17-18: Stocking stitch yarn B
8. Row 19: *K2Btog, rep from * to end (14sts)
9. Row 20: * P2Btog, rep from * to end (7sts)
10. Row 21: *K1B, K2Btog, rep once more K1B
11. Row 22: P2Btog, P2Btog, P1B (3sts)

12. Make a 10 row I cord using yarn C.

13. Sew side seams and fold the I- cord in half to make a loop at the top and join it to the crown.

Ruched Egg Cosy

This ruched egg cosy is based on the classical vintage Tea Cosy. Each section is made with 8 metres of yarn divided into 4m lengths.

1. Using 5mm needles and yarn A cast on 42sts.
2. Foundation row (only if using the traditional cast on method), ktbl.
3. Row 1 (RS): S1, *K4 using 1st strand yarn A, K4 using 2nd strand yarn A, repeat from* to last stitch, K1 using strand A.
4. Row 2: Sl 1 * K4, bring the second strand of yarn to the front, and take the 1st strand to the back of work, K4, rep from * to last st, take the 2nd strand of yarn to the back of work, and bring the 1st strand of yarn to the front, K1
5. These two rows form the basic pattern
6. Now work in 4 row stripes repeating the two row pattern twice with each colour
7. Rows 3-6: As rows 1 -2 with yarn B
8. Rows 7-10: As rows 1-4 with yarn A
9. Rows 11-14: As rows 1-2 with yarn B
10. Rows 15-18: As rows 1-4 with yarn A
11. Rows 19-20: As rows 1-2 with yarn B
12. Row 21: Sl 1* K2tog, K2tog using strand A, rep from * to last st using strand B, K1 strand A (22sts)
13. Row 22: Work ruching as row 2 over each set of 2 sts.
14. Cut off yarn B
15. Row 23: Work as row 1 decreasing each section of 2 down to 1 stitch. (11sts)
16. Row 24: As row 2, working each section of 1 stitch.
17. Row 25: K2tog x5, K1
18. Complete as Bobble egg cosy.

Other books by Monica Russel include:

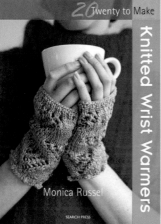

All the titles, kits and the yarns for these projects can be ordered from Monica's website:

www.theknitknacks.co.uk